ALISON BRACKENBURY was b[   ] s
educated at St Hugh's College [   ] -
tershire. She has just retired frc [   ] ♪
business. She has published seven previous collections with Carcanet,
and a *Selected Poems*. Her work has received an Eric Gregory Award
and a Cholmondeley Award.

Also by Alison Brackenbury from Carcanet Press

1829
After Beethoven
Breaking Ground
Bricks and Ballads
Christmas Roses
Dreams of Power
Selected Poems
Singing in the Dark

ALISON BRACKENBURY

Then

CARCANET

First published in Great Britain in 2013 by
Carcanet Press Limited
Alliance House
Cross Street
Manchester M2 7AQ

www.carcanet.co.uk

A CIP catalogue record for this book is available from the British Library

ISBN 978 1 84777 118 6

The publisher acknowledges financial assistance from Arts Council England

Typeset by XL Publishing Services, Exmouth
Printed and bound in England by SRP Ltd, Exeter

Contents

The Trent rises, 1947   9
Bath cubes   10
Translated   11
The shepherd's son's photo-album   12
Great–great–   14
I.O.W.   15
Edith leaves   16
Home leave   17
Frayed   18
Left   19
Binder twine   20
Ditches   21
The lunch box   22
Köchel 622   23
Suddenly   24
After the funeral   25
Fruit in February   26
On a February night   27
Out of the wood   28
On guard   29
The shed   30
At eighty   31
Giving way   32
Your signature is required   33
On the aerial   34
Leap year   35
Serena speaks of February   36
Lapwings   37
Victoria Coach Station, 11 p.m.   38
St Kilda's wren   39
'Song, though, is a uniquely human business'   40
To Mr W.S., from his agent   41
Too late   42
A quiet night   43
Leaving Cheltenham   44
Late at Long Eaton   46
Money   47

I want life to be more like poetry   48
Glazed over   49
Dessert   50
May Day, 1972   51
The cricket   52
Before breakfast   53
Bombus   54
Asleep   55
The second jab   56
The Shackleton expedition   57
In the Black Country   58
The Shaker chair   59
Near Russell Square   60
November 11th   61
The First Emperor   62
The Wallace Collection   63
Thermal   64
Diary of a stretcher bearer   65
Stubbs and the horse   66
John Wesley's horse   67
Rosie   68
Take off   69
Harvest   70
In an August garden   71
At Needlehole   72
The nymph considers the garden   73
The jobbing welder   74
The button factory in Bologna   75
The Beatles in Hamburg   76
Mentioned in Minnesota   77
Getting up   78
Wilfred Owen at the Advanced Horse Transport Depot, 1917   79
5 a.m.   80
First   81
The twenty-ninth of December   82
Looking for the cat   83
In store   84
Flood
    1. Flood   87
    2. Mitchell   88

3. Bowsers   89
4. Litres   90
5. Switched on   91
6. Review   92
No   93

Acknowledgements   94

The Trent rises, 1947

When you heard the water whisper
in Crown Yard and Sailors' Alley,
when your husband saw the river
no longer lazy – swollen, free;
what did you grab, to take with you upstairs?
What would I take with me?

Would I snatch letters from the flood,
so their clearest lines and kisses
did not meet condoms, tampons, mud?
Save bills? Saucepans? Water misses
no hidden, plastered wire. No kettle could
boil. The fusebox hisses.

Computers, in a leaky boat?
They hauled fresh water, tins. The swell
of river made the hall a moat.
Tortoise to bucket! Chickens fell
into their bath. Aboard the Co-op's milk float,
the pigs raised merry hell.

Bath cubes

Lily of the valley, Devon violet, English rose
brought crumpled foil, white silk's swirl, the gurgled names of those
great-aunts and godmothers, Edie, Phil and Gwen,
like the coarse white bath cubes, which will not come again

with harsh and gritty powder, oiled steam, the after-reek,
jasmine sliding past the river fish (then few) who did not speak.
I measured them like love, a flowering of the self,
not the final desperate present plucked quickly from the shelf

which no one told me then. No one ever told my toes,
creased and flushed from chilling water as the bathroom window
                                                    froze,
lost in mists of fake French lavender, false lilac, summer rose.

Translated

Yet all I took from it was words.
How strange! It was a solid place.
Potatoes, like an old man's face,
clay-caked, fell ruddy from the spade.
Huge sheep, the fruit-crammed pies they made,
now dwindle like the summer's birds.

What did they say? 'It's fairing up.'
My grandfather, his hot blue eyes
pure Viking, watched clouds sweep from skies.
His younger son said 'last back end'
for autumn, leafless, with no friend.
Silent, I stirred my steaming cup.

My mother sighed. They would not fit:
old words, new money. In my head
I hear what Margaret Thatcher said,
puzzling note-takers. MPs bayed,
she lost taught tones, Hansard's 'afraid',
shrieked, to our schoolyard, 'I'm not frit!'

The shepherd's son's photo-album

I could show you sad stories
as bright shy children peep
by wind-bent trees, grey ditches,
in crippled love that keeps

the girl a kitchen shadow
with fine hair, crooked teeth,
who, when brain tumours seize her,
rages into sleep.

The quick one fails all papers,
sits still, as clocks strike; eats.
But two work hard; one marries.
Here are the three fat sheep.

You laugh till pages quiver:
three perfect spheres with fleece
washed soft and deep as pom-poms,
three full moons stuffed with swedes.

They fill the narrow hill-lane
as marchers crowd a street.
They peer at us like judges.
They float on tiny feet.

Lined up with dangling nose ropes
they calmly wait their feast.
Only one glances sideways.
Beware a knowing beast.

Here I am, dandled. Orphaned lambs
strain to their bottles, deep
in rough grass by my smiling aunt
who has no child to keep.

My grandmother, in her long coat,
frowns till the ram stands meek.
Her youngest waves his camera
before his mind finds sleep.

My grandfather, his tallest son,
grasp ribbons, cups to keep.
Gone, gone. All waste. And yet they laugh.
Here are the three fat sheep.

Great-great-

I own your desk, Eliza, with your story,
the black-spined Bible with your flourished entry.
Your husband, our last farmer, dead at forty
took off the farm of crooked apple trees,

white pail upon the table in our picture.
But you moved on, with your plain kindly daughters
who settled down to marry their farm labourers.
Louisa's anxious child was my grandmother,

Louisa died, bee-stung. Your *Ls* grew dashing,
lodged by the North Sea, mornings calm, nights lashing.
Life is before and after. Breath hides passion.
Your jet braids jutted out in reckless fashion.

Why did you give my grandmother the Bible,
your last girl's youngest child, as in a fable?
Did you tip your black ink across this table?
I stroke its pool. I wish I was still able

to ask her of you, where small coals would glint
the desk in shepherds' kitchens. She was sent
on trips for an old woman, strangely bent,
to village shops, which sold gunpowder then

which the old woman spooned out, smiled, despatched
each twist, rammed up the flue. Awed children watched
soots fall like rain, black laughter I can catch.
What good can one desk do? Give me your match.

I.O.W.

I have seen China, in its deepest cold,
Russia, where each platform showed for sale
a samovar, a soldier's coat unrolled.
In Kenya, I heard lions breathe through the night
behind thin skin of tents. Now stiff and grey
I check late ferries for the Isle of Wight

which I saw once, once only, a faint smudge
my eyes strained after, from a darkened beach.
What does it hold? More beaches I could trudge,
Victoria's house at Osborne, a brick city
where grief could wander down the garden walks,
a ledge of time, above fringed shawls and pity.

My mother's mother went there as a maid.
Her employer sailed into summer
a rented home, too small, so that she stayed
in lodgings' freedom. But in later life
her hips failed, she grew heavy as a cliff.
She dragged across small stones, a bitter wife.

Three days before the stroke, she dreamed she ran
her village fields, frost's willows circling near,
deep ponds she dodged. I will sail, while I can,
with one light case, across the dark, slow water,
stand on the small beach; see my grandmother
walking the wet sand with the coachman's daughter.

Edith leaves

There she was, my Aunt Edie, going off to service,
scared, and fourteen, crying
by the side of the train.
She did not want to be a maid,
but to run straight back to the cottage,
to her grim red mother, to the tall bean row
where her taller father waited.

So he, in his labourer's best boots, climbed
with her on the train, then travelled
to the next brief stop
(could he pay? was he caught?),
jumped down. She sat, still crying.

How did he reach home? I know. He walked,
the lanes smoked dust. He did not see
the hawthorn's fresh and spicy leaves,
cream, heavy heads of elder.

'What use was that?' her mother said.
'You could have ridden all the way
and she would still be crying.'

What would you be, as the train shook by,
as the pollens stroked his shoulder,
the flowering may, with its neat chopped thorn,
the heady, weeping elder?

Home leave

After the wars, they drifted back
to their limestone village, perched on clay.
A Crimean veteran with one leg
lodged in his two rooms, did not pay
till the Earl's crooked agent came
and made him sign his rights away.

After the war, I knew the man,
dapper beneath the Legion's lamps,
the trimmest dancer, on the beat,
untouched by floor's dust, our sweat's damps.
No one crossed him. He would explode,
back in the jungle prison camp.

My grandfather had three numbers,
battalions turned to mud, before
his son was sent to Palestine,
pulled home, heard gunfire from the shore.
I saw shops close, cars crowd, skies warm.
And then I left, before the war.

Frayed

On the grey rug, now on our workshop chair,
I sprawled on rough grass forty years back, where
I read my father's paper's huge headlines.
'Profumo'. Who? I had not heard before
of swimming pools, the young red-headed whore.
By the lorry driver's house, where no one swore,
capitals roared black: 'MINISTER RESIGNS'.

I fold the blanket. All did not go well
amongst us. Families keep rooms in hell.
I wind my way out by a long tough thread;
ride by rich farms. The labourers' widows say
'That's where that Mandy Davies used to stay',
who threw truth, rough as blankets, in our way.
'Well, he *would* say that, wouldn't he?' she said.

Left

They never sang to me.
Since they no longer stride the hill
or peg out creaking washing
they never will.

Grandmother's mother's desk
from the legendary lost farm
was salvaged by my parents
from dog food, sheep salves, grime.

They found, stuffed in the deep drawers,
penny notebooks. Letters were
traced airily, as spider-thin
as young Victoria.

Until a dashing black hand:
for sheep thrush, baby scour,
horse worming balls, from fenugreek,
saltpetre, elderflower.

What's this? 'I am a lady bright,
my love has listed, gone.
What care I for world or treasure?'
It is a song

which I will sing, flat, softly,
to great moon's glow, cold week.
The next page lists the lambs lost,
white sulphur, fenugreek.

Binder twine

What is it? Nothing fancy. Plastic string,
pulled from high machines at harvest's ending,
it winds round packed straw-bales, the softer hay,
with daisy, dock, the deadly ragwort, hiding.

I grew up next to farms, trespassed on stacks,
hauled twine to jump the bales' yawning cracks.
Thirty years in town, still thralled to horses,
I pull its stiff snakes from the rusting racks

to tie gates, bind horse-rugs. With stronger skeins
the farmer fixed his chimney. In North Wales
they call its knots and webs 'Radnorshire welding'
which made my father laugh in his sad age.

Each year spills different colour, rich on yards.
We did not like the red, too stiff and hard –
I chose the lemon, with its silky edge
which faded into white, beneath stern stars.

When this horse dies, I will heave stable doors
no more. Yet coils of twine will hide for years
in pockets, sheds. Curled quiet as moss, it is
the line I haul through darkness. What is yours?

Ditches

Still they lie deep, though I have gone,
the great dykes with their glinting load,
brown winter floods, fields' wasteful run,
planted too soon. Are there machines
which rear and dip from the firm road,
scoop glistening banks, clear rotted leaves?

Yet still, I know, there is a day –
a stone-blocked pipe, a tumbled tree –
when a man slides down with a spade,
beats back dead nettles, elders' switch,
sunk from the sky as under sea,
digs, sweats and clears the gurgling ditch.

As we drove down the empty road,
swept round the only bend for miles
my father drowned the lorry's noise,
told me a ditcher, working well,
sliced the dyke's wall, unhomed a rat
which squealed and bit him as it fell.

He caught the fever they called 'Weels'
(though now I know the name is 'Weil's').
The ambulance flashed past the drowned fields,
too late. For to this day, a man
can die from rats, as in the floods
of Bangladesh or Vietnam.

Then, by the only bend for miles,
smooth lawn flowed round a bungalow.
The farm's young shipwrecked wife filled hours
gardening bikini'd. Calm and rich
this sunlit girl – the story goes –
sent several drivers in the ditch.

The lunch box

Though my mother is dying, you buy vegetarian cheese.
There is celery – did you grow it? The rolls are sliced twice,
wrapped in plastic, then foil. They must have taken hours.
I nibble them on the coach. I keep the paper napkin
with all its frantic flowers.

Köchel 622

Yes. I see why he preferred the clarinet,
as my mother hunches, eyes closed, yet
intent on tapes for her own funeral.

The clarinet is darker. Mud and oil
have touched it; how he died, sick in a bowl;
morphine; the steady heating of the seas,
pale silk unwrinkled by a plump girl's knees,
the plunging horse, loose in a winter field,
the white perfumes a ripe lychee will yield,
long nights. Dull days. The goldfinch and the hawk,
the dance of breath which washes out our talk,
spin on the wind. Above the tug of root,
yes, I know why I still prefer the flute.

Suddenly

'It's the season,' I said, 'the temperature.'
'No,' they said patiently, 'it's cancer,
it makes no difference.' But tides tug.
The birds' water froze, then re-froze, all heat spent.
As I swerved round the vans on the darkening road
the light took her, and she went.

After the funeral

White lights flow north. Red lights fade south.
The great road runs glittering under the bridge.

As my mother's lists had every act planned
I had heard her music; not the blackbird's
whose lilt cut the air between hissed tapes and words.
Only the wind fled. His flat heavy land
dragged her, unwillingly. Dancer's small feet
shuffled, then swelled, every shadowed room neat.

Lovers or family? Boots or clean floor?
I rode one horse, the strong bay, with great heart.
From letters, reproaches, cold years spent apart,
came to their scrubbed blinds, strange plants by their door,
cried 'I saw a heron, close to the train' –
from dazzle of sun which will drink us again.

She sat up at nights, coquettish and wild
in feasts with my father, slept out the day,
pushed the strong sun and the strangers away.
I know her no more than I did as a child,
her damage, her dreams. It springs into me
with rush of the dark, that we are both free.

I count all the bridges. Here is the fourth.
Red lights stream south. White lights flow north.

Fruit in February

My mother dead. What did she leave?
Dry days of frost, a weight to grieve.
The dead wake us with worries,
sour milk, the universe.

The hedge beneath the house was thick
with fruit, which gave the glow of milk,
the child's dream. She snatched fingers,
mother's nightmare: 'Pois-on-ous.'

Birth, death, we sleep from dream to dream.
Beside my path to work, a gleam;
the same bush; the shadowed house,
though birds shout, traffic murmurs.

No, these small globes are not pure light
but crazed with brown. Flaws hurt her sight.
The dead leave us their worries,
white fruit for birds, snowberries.

On a February night

Bats slept in the tall house, the one she loved,
in sash cords' gaps. My sister hated them.
My father drove them out. Look how they rise,
in clouds of voices, leaf for winter trees.

Out of the wood

I save these things to give to you:
that young beech leaves are breaking through
on sapling trees; not on the old
whose buds stay pointed, sealed, as closed
as was my mother, from the cold.
Pouched flower, the dead man's finger, gleams,
mauve orchids fly from speckled leaves.

You bring the small things to tell me,
the talk you had on the last tee,
how cowslips spread from the one spot,
ants carry seeds in nodded lines,
a queen wasp found your compost; not
how you love night, when none need part,
or how the great pain gripped your heart.

On guard

My father, aged nineteen, tramps Düsseldorf,
no tourist, guards the military HQ,
brown curls crammed in his cap, gun scoured, in view
as the top brass roars into Düsseldorf,
raw shrapnel in his neck, false teeth on gums,
from forests where the wild boar fled from guns.

At night the staff cars sweep from Düsseldorf.
Past the stone houses, down the cobbled street
the Sergeant Major limps on stockinged feet,
'Don't shoot, you bloody fool!' as Düsseldorf
freezes, my father's rifle trains his head,
his rations heap a hungry Fräulein's bed.

What, in the icy dawn of Düsseldorf,
shoots a sharp rustle from the broken hedge?
The sentry, bruised, sprawls in the gutter's edge.
A German Shepherd, Nazi Düsseldorf's,
breathes over him. Instructed once to trip,
now starving, she remembered her old trick,

awaits his orders. Whistled, in hills' white space
through frost, low sun, his father's sheepdogs race,
soft Toots, quick Choc. She licks his frozen face.

The shed

He looked after tools, not just his own,
palm-polished handles, Victorian elm,
stamped with initials for John Maidens Barnes

my grandmother's father, who never bought farms,
but his own clutch of ditch-tools. Reach down the hoe

a blacksmith beat for the left-handed twist
of his father, the shepherd, who weeded bean rows
in after-work dazzle, the pipe's long blue mist.

How far they have travelled. This death is still raw.
Shallots' small worlds, held by knots of string,

spin as I brush them. I unhook the fork
he had wiped clean. Soil's finest grains cling.
Though I know it is sun, swept through glass, over land,

the handle grips hot as his palm to my hand.

At eighty

Spanker, Sharper, Prince and Bob
were horses that my father drove
through rain, through clay, down car-free roads
the workless tramped, for his first job.

He told me as we waited, bored,
outside my dozing mother's ward
Bob kicked him sailing down the yard.

Bob also bolted from the tree,
dragged with clanked chain. The closest shave
came when he swayed back, peacefully,

legs tapping Spanker's sun-warm side,
back to the hay, from dinner break.
The great grey Belgian reared beside,

horse, cart, crashed toppling like a tree.
The shaft's kink saved his battered sides.
Six Irish shearers dragged him free.

A bungalow's quiet bedroom took
breath neither weight nor war could rob.
Out of the dark with patient feet
came Spanker, Sharper, Prince and Bob.

Giving way

As oil, like honey, dripped down grating plates,
coaxes the engine's breath from growl to purr,
as pure white tablets smooth the battered burr
inside my hips, so I can march up hills,
so that quick wave, because a driver waits
behind the parked vans, in a narrow gap,
the wedged-in stranger nodding, smiling back,
drops courtesy, as when a thrush-song spills

into the traffic. So my father waved,
short countryman turned driver, stiff as clay,
fierce mother waiting at the close of day
by scrubbed floors, army gloss on every boot.
We rarely met; so little has been saved,
dredged from those lives. But when a stranger brakes,
when I edge on, my hand, turned stiff too, makes
straight-fingered like a soldier, his salute.

Your signature is required

Oh reading wills I mourn them:
my father's upright hand,
careful from the village school.
So his father wrote; his mother
shaped child's letters, crimped like pastry,
pinched, like the cowslip's petal.
Who will write like that again?
And then, her zeros,
more trouble than a pleasure,
lawyer's chill trick, a second will,
the day my mother slept.

But the tax is saved. I sign
in my slanted dashing hand.
I walk the broad path, common,
to the hill we do not own.
The bramble's flowers raise storms,
palest golds, rough creams and browns,
the gatekeepers, the butterflies
of hottest harsh July.

So I know that they are safe,
so, forgetting them, I pass
a C of moon so tender
she must not be glimpsed through glass.

On the aerial

Starling is numerous, holds in his throat
the many colours of his oily coat.
Each year he – like his fathers – finds new noise,
wolf-whistles tall as boys,
the phone's trill, then the shriek
of Kirsty, loudest child in all our street.
Tonight he softly mews. Then through his voice are poured
jay, blackbird's honey, thrush–lilts. He, half-heard,
tilts at faint stars, is Spring, is every bird.

Leap year

In February, in the dark time
from pancakes' smoke to Easter's shine

in Friday's rush, at ten to four,
a driver tapped our workshop door,

turned to the truck. I heard high wind
whistle the cliffs of flats behind.

I went to prop our own door wide.
He was a small man, heavy-eyed,

who spoke of rain, leaned in his truck.
I saw the great steel door blow back,

sweep at him like a guillotine.
I shouted. He leapt back in time.

'It would have crushed his spine, his head.
He would have died,' my husband said.

Instead, he carried trays of screws,
drove off inside the roar of news.

The twenty-ninth, the lightless west,
rained on my face. I stood, was blessed.

Serena speaks of February

'At least the sun will shine on both sides of the hedge,'
the small woman says to me. Her son-in-law died from drugs,
her daughter invents her children's names, a recklessness I admire.
Now she lives in town. But she is peering in the hedge,
and I can see it too. The hawthorn buds glint red,
the chaffinch, who pinks and flirts, is redder still.
The sun is soaring. Though we will not come back,
on both sides of the high hedge, the sun will.

Lapwings

They were everywhere. No. Just God or smoke
is that. They were the backdrop to the road,

my parents' home, the heavy winter fields
from which they flashed and kindled and uprode

the air in dozens. I ignored them all.
'What are they?' 'Oh – peewits – ' Then a hare flowed,

bounded the furrows. Marriage. Child. I roamed
round other farms. I only knew them gone

when, out of a sad winter, one returned.
I heard the high mocked cry 'Pee – *wit*', so long

cut dead. I watched it buckle from vast air
to lure hawks from its chicks. That time had gone.

Gravely, the parents bobbed their strip of stubble.
How had I let this green and purple pass?

Fringed, plumed heads (full name, the crested plover)
fluttered. So crowned cranes stalk Kenyan grass.

Then their one child, their anxious care, came running,
squeaked along each furrow, dauntless, daft.

Did I once know the story of their lives,
do they migrate from Spain? or coasts' cold run?

And I forgot their massive arcs of wing.
When their raw cries swept over, my head spun

With all the brilliance of their black and white
As though you cracked the dark and found the sun.

Victoria Coach Station, 11 p.m.

Two girls stumble, drunken friends.
'Going *now*? Where's our vodka?'

They drag out matching scarves,
baguettes, crumbs' silk.
                              As if on ice,

claws skid, beaks bob. How I love pigeons,
filthy, joy-filled, precise.

St Kilda's wren

I thought you said 'rain'. You said wren,
small haunter of bog and lichen,
loud as gulls' laughter, fierce as men.

Let me guess. Who was St Kilda?
Housewife? Healer? Abbey builder?
Or a man? The rain blows wilder,

on to the railway bank. The bird
flits down, swollen, small brown word.
The male, who wove each nest, is heard

shrilled, triumphant, darts up when
other birds shrink from storm or fen,
shouts to the saintless. Rain, wren, wren.

'Song, though, is a uniquely human business'

(Don Paterson, Poetry Review, *Summer 2007)*

Have you told the blackbird
who wanders air
on walnuts by the yard
the rough farm where
pines sigh above the gun's reach, or
in lilacs by our workshop's broken door?

As the sparks leap and fade
he tries and trails
a note, a run, a glide,
as one sun fails
he steals, then builds; long runs; a phrase
from brother's, father's, grandfather's lit days.

He will not cough or croup,
he pours each note,
lost trees, each sweep and swoop
gold from his throat.
Idle in sun, pierces dawn's sky
high as the rain's rush. Song? Blackbird, reply.

To Mr W.S., from his agent

The sonnets were a flop. But plagues are over.
Go back to plays again! Don't be cast down.
Plots aren't your strength. Steal one! A fight, a murder.
And this time, please, a good part for the clown.

Too late

There is a dark and hungry hour
before this bed
when nothing is awake
but owls, hedgehogs, bats and deer,
drivers and nurses watch their dials flicker;
lovers; the yawning engineer
patient as porridge, after storms have torn
through power-lines, must twist and test each wire,
till pylons heave and crackle
before dawn.

A quiet night

'Dear Mohini', I typed, at one a.m.,
then all the furniture rattled upstairs
as though you flung our shared things everywhere,
in some midnight fit. The floor rose then.
It heaved like a horse, shook low ceilings, my chair.
No lorries or juddered goods train could make
solid bones shudder. This was an earthquake:

I held my breath. The lamp, my yellow moon,
blurred for five seconds with the aftershock,
poised on the table's edge, it did not drop.
All stilled to silence. Would more quakes come soon?
Were trains safe in our cutting, though trees rocked?
I did not rush outside, up to your touch.
I tapped, 'Mohini,
                  Thank you very much.'

Leaving Cheltenham

One day, as now, my bus will come.
It slides out in the yawning sun.
I see a building with no name

on the north corner of the street
where bookmakers and chip shops meet.
It was the Odeon, where we came

to dusty crimson by thick doors,
you in flounced skirts you wore at four.
We watched the jiving, dashing cats

whose baby grand rocked more and more,
who dropped, still singing, floor by floor,
who landed with a flick of hats.

It was so warm and dark, a dream
of sunlit endings, spooned ice-cream
still hard as ice-floes by reels' hiss.

I did not want you a rich fool
in shuttered rooms, a blazered school.
I told you, life is not like this.

Then life obligingly showed teeth.
It struck you early, with close death,
the rough school hemmed you like a pack,

so each day was a prison yard
you would not leave. It left you scarred.
Hurt, angry, you will not go back.

Not to the Odeon, for sure.
The sleek seal-girl above the door
is gone, its windows crazed. Then night

brakes the bus by the smashed tree's piles,
no smooth cut here: reversed, wet miles,
black film, shock ending. I was right.

Late at Long Eaton

How views from idling trains show lives
in cuttings, where long gardens wind
down to the rails, or dark canals.
There each home's narrow kingdom tells
what is most loved; a trampoline
lifts children, where all trees have been
ruthlessly felled. A table stands
with kissing chairs for late-night friends.
You urge me, love the human race.
But leave, past rail and bank, a space
where I may let rich ivies run,
flowered nettles' lemon trails breathe sun,
young robins flit, the sharp wrens cry,
the Speckled Wood's new-hatched wings dry
which tremble, taste the wide air, fly.

Money

Where did it come from? Sugar bags
my grandmother packed damp with dust
scraped from the coalshed's whitewashed must
to flare cheap flames through salvaged logs.

What made it grow? The careful books
of maths and verbs my mother frowned
above; long days which weighed her down,
then pensions' goldrush, huge as tax.

Where should it go? The chandelier
hovered. The suited boy could see
a five-year bond from AIG,
insurers to America.

Although coaldust weighs constantly,
pencil does not fade, houses fell
unsold. The lenders gazed on hell.
'Tottering times for AIG.'

What should I do? Advisers, scent
swaddling them from the plunging screen,
foresaw the final rescue plan.
I own the US government.

World crisis stalls. I work on. Slow
as those stilled hands, I count, then pack
screws, shipping bills. Small doors edge black
where money comes from, where we go.

I want life to be more like poetry

(Pete Doherty)

Poetry will not hold your hand,
drop down her face to kiss you.
Poetry makes no midnight calls
to cry how she will miss you.
Poetry cannot run the street
to check that you are there;
nor close your eyes, then turn, then breathe
lilac on slow air.

Glazed over

I hand him the seeds in a gold-rimmed pot,
once crammed with glacé cherries.
'My mother loved these, ate them with a spoon,
they had her arrested on honeymoon,

just after the war.' She packed one tiny pot,
sugar lust, scarlet cherries,
the innocent gift of a friend, while hacked
wives' limbs lay dumped on luggage racks.

A traveller saw ooze, so red, like a shout,
slow sticky leak of cherries.
Plucked by police from the platform,
they ran, to their landlady's curling ham.

'I hate them,' he says, though he takes the pot;
'I will only eat fresh cherries.'
He sweeps away in his company's car.
The placard flaps, on the March wind, WAR.

His wild daughter sits up all night.
From her dead-end job and takeaway food
she flashes through stations of murder and blood.
She loves maraschino cherries.

Dessert

The gooseberry bush hung down the wall
by the slow Fifties' summer sun,
the rundown cottage. After wars
Italian farm workers had come.
A widow, child-high, in black clothes
lodged there. Did she see them fall,

the gooseberries' pale globes of gold?
I reached for them in heat or rain,
aged eight. One fruit would fill my mouth.
It was the sun, to blind small pains,
the perfect note, the dreamed-of south,
then, to my grandmother. Housebound, old,

she left us; that shawled lady, too.
There is a chance rough berries spill
in leaping hands, still spiced by theft,
above new walls, on that small hill.
This shop has one box, ripe yet left,
dusked fruits, lit amber. They will do.

May Day, 1972

How gold it was, the first wash of sky
as voices floated from the tower
as you spun the umbrella the tourists loved,
on every spike a paper flower.

How cold it was at the day's mid-point
when tiredness kicked in like a mule
when you stood at work and the hours stretched
as sea in fog's breath, tense and dull.

How rich and dark was the crumb of cake
which came from the tin of the dancing men
in absurd white clothes: for luck, new life.
How nothing was the same again.

The cricket

You wished, you wished, you wished in vain.
The August wedding stung with rain.
The dreadful mother lived too long.
The business shrank from his first dream
to crumpled bills at one a.m.
The child said 'See you!' then was gone.

Gaze in the garden's tiny sphere:
you thought it was the hedgehog's year,
who snuffled plates. Mating or killed,
he disappeared. And butterflies?
Only one peacock's sun-filled eyes
at noon. But when dusk's breath was held

there crouched, upon the roses' bank,
bronze grasshopper, a tiny tank.
The metal wings were not for fight.
Three more, as by a southern sea,
whirred, clinked and throbbed, sang constantly,
gave all you wished, through August's night.

Before breakfast

All confidence, the fox wheels to the road.
But I step forward. There are guns abroad.
So he is gone, for foxes only turn
as wind can pass, as oxygen can burn,
he flickers, shadow in the morning sun,
poised by the cutting's height. Then he is gone,
cold sleeper underground, brush marks on plate,
sharp bark from nowhere, as I read too late.

Bombus

In unkempt borders whose sweet mess
the plumber calls 'floriferous'
the bumbles are a distant drone,
ear's soothing, irritating home.
Bees grow rare, as the heat soars. Look –
antennae, species, crowd the book.

Huge white- and buff-tailed trundle by
trumpeted shrubs in January.
Rough, golden-backed, the carder bee
scrambles rose pollens through July.
In fuchsia's tunnels, a long eye,
bombus hortorum, garden bee,

gleams warning (while sleek bees of hives
fly tame). These follow hidden lives
in old mouse-nests, a crumbling wall.
Startled, you let the fat book fall.
Bee booms, black bomber, at your face,
too wild for sun's grace, or for rhyme.

Asleep

The deer rest in the barley's waves.
They glimpse my horse, another deer?
her belly cream-flashed, eyes, black caves.
I squint. One stag's branched antlers lift
(so snow moose rise, from Sweden's drifts).
Wind blurs and breaks the barley near.

The deer are roe. Their long backs range
from honeyed brown of last year's fawns
to richest black. The corn's silks plunge.
What flicks the barley's whiskers? Tails?
I watch green wind till my sight fails.
Five heads fly up, a wood of horns.

My torn foot swells inside its boot.
The doctor gives me yellow pills.
When I lie down, my head's sky floods
with pulsing brown, a muddy rose,
gas clouds, star-breath. A dream flows
of when the high trees clothed the hills.

A boy steps out. He knows the deer,
their order, till the stag's first death.
They crowd behind him without fear.
He tells me their most secret names,
light as wind, sharp as barley grains.
I wake to dream the deer's warm breath.

The second jab

Never have I kept such a wild kitten,
one of eight, born in a tiny house.
With carpet rolls and sun, she spun, then hissed
as paper bags go down, at slightest touch.
Then she grew milder, clawed along my skirt,
fell spilled across my arm, asleep, like water;
floated, as we swim, unborn or dead.

I found her in the wake of several deaths
just as the sunlight sharpened to the cold
though trees refused to turn. Can kindness kill?
She had injections that her first poor owner
could not have paid for, drugs to keep her well.
Now when I pick her up she strikes at me,
fills the warm rooms with one long keen of pain.

I crouch, in soft skirts, dressed for my London trip,
to laugh with friends. 'Go. I will cope,' you say.
Surely she will not die? Will she be well?
I do not know. Day drops me through its skin
to the dark place. I climb up coach steps, smile.
How love can tear, and binds us to the wild.
A useless name. 'Shadow,' I say. 'Oh Shadow.'

The Shackleton expedition

The ship is trapped in ice,
the ship is trapped in snow.
A carpenter with curly hair
nurses his cat below.

The captain counts the rations.
A handpicked group will go
in one small boat. The rest will wait
islanded in snow.

Lists and stores lie under
the captain's focused eye.
The siege is just beginning.
All animals must die.

Their boat drives through. Each man survives
the ice, the breath of glass.
The captain could be hero
if he were upper class.

The curly-headed carpenter,
old in his Glasgow flat,
wakes every day to hate the man
who shot his tabby cat.

In the Black Country

for Roy Palmer

Brush the sooted trees at Cradley,
tramp the ironworks' ash at Brierley,
taste the coal-dust, swirled
round pitheads for the Earl of Dudley
whose miners stole for weekend loot
bronze pheasants from the airy woods
my grandfather helped pen for shoots,
another world.

Visitors plucked one branch of hell.
Gas seeped, ropes snapped, the bad seam fell
on John Dawes, twenty-three.
Women in sackcloth swore as well
as miners. Clean, in the chain shop,
they watched the anvil, levered up
bar for the hammer's perfect drop,
iron like toffee.

Songs, then strikes, then deportations:
praise all who risked for fair conditions,
all who took part.
Smog lifts from China's power stations.
Who was the girl who sat alone
high on the coach, watched chimneys loom,
who cried for joy, since this was home?
Oh my black heart.

The Shaker chair

They were the strangest sect.
Their founder's marriage had
turned, fist and boot, to bad.
To the New World she fled
with the white-clothed elect,
each to a single bed.

I think that this is true.
Their hymn lilts through my head,
its beat strikes their light tread
as they left each night's halls,
men, women, filed from view
separate. No hot dark falls

with their sure dancers' feet.
Did they keep horses too,
coax stones from hooves, comb through
the burdocked forelock? Cars
rushed past them. Silent, neat,
they faded like dawn stars.

Their furniture stays perfect.
Which is the pale wood?
Beech, ash, each curve made good
by unstroked hands, sways there,
slow music was that sect.
Sit gently on their chair.

Near Russell Square

Round old corners, in new London,
party-bound, push back a door
to see a ramp steep as a hill,
dark as rain, a cobbled floor
up which you hobble, in sleek boots,
teetering, about to fall.
How did cab horses heave these curves?
This is the Horse Hospital.

What drugs or scalpels waited them
before the cart came round for meat?
Great beaten tie-rings mount the walls.
Bricks herring-bone the drinkers' feet.
Girls mention them, before they laugh,
shy from the bar's buzz, bottles' rank,
cross the bare room with tiny swerves
as though they dodged a nose, a flank.

Small windows mist. Who rode the cabs?
The lawyer, ruin in his case,
girls with a braided purse of hope,
the child who cried to school's barred days,
lovers, changing disillusion
for one more; unheard, too near,
the horse, whose lameness jarred each stride,
led up the slippery slopes, came here.

Now engines purr, the horse is pet,
why do we not tear down these walls
whose dark and quiet is animal?
Botch, mend, grab reins before a fall?
The hay is dust that was so sweet,
the world is work, the moon is gone.
New steel-tipped heels clip frozen streets.
Behind, the cab heaves, rattles on.

November 11th

Now I recall the dead, before the gun,
hollow in our soggy park, will summon
this small town's silence. What would they have done?

First they would slip, then curse this greasy rain,
England's long winter damp, where joints creak pain.
They might cram crates, flit suddenly to Spain,

sink rosé, fight. For emptied of their lead
they are not saints, their work, their wheels' skid
reckless as ours. They might, again, be dead.

No, let them live, swear, fidget for the sun,
talk to a passing girl, as I have done,
by her wet tapping heels, fine, feathered hair,
stand startled at the echo of the gun.

The First Emperor

He made the many kingdoms one,
he tore men from the land,
forced China to one neat small script
no peasant understands.
Clay soldiers crowd to guard his grave,
good weapons in dead hands.

Did he choke scholars live in pits?
The scholars disagree.
He longed to fight for ever, sipped
potions of mercury.
Died on the eastern frontier, as
a hawk falls, suddenly.

His sons were swept away before
the slaughtered clerks turned earth.
Mao praised him. What were borders, weights,
that deadly fine script worth?
Girls ache in factories still to give
clay soldiers rapid birth.

A peasant scrabbling for a well
found broken hands, criss-crossed.
Scratches on slips of pots name those
who slept in the kilns' dust.
The peasant's brown face smiles at me.
The Emperor's face is lost.

The Wallace Collection

Not house, but jewel box. The first Duke
built it so he could blast at duck
in the dim marshes. Buses roar.
Who bought the art? Earls five and four.

The last, though loathed, crony to kings,
outbid frantically at auction,
left landscape's blues, Our Lady's face,
forgotten in their packing case,
then died. His secretary, stunned,
found he was heir, the unclaimed son.

What filled the rooms? China's glazed glow,
bleu lapis, bleu céleste, bleu beau,
the last French queen's last desk, where clouds
of lilies swim the water's wood,
leafed with frail holly she could slam
when servants padded through her room.

Rococo gilt hides mercury.
Gilders, best paid, were first to die.
By Chelsea's lights the river smells.
Art draws, withdraws, bankrupts, compels.
The good son left to us the best
fine hands had formed, rough hands possessed,
bleu beau, bleu lapis, bleu céleste.

The '*bleus*' are the names of several generations of blue glaze for Sèvres
porcelain.

Thermal

Sulis Minerva, they found your stone head
in Bath, where my daughter drove me today,
half-Roman, half-Celt. Do not lecture. Instead
we wade through blue pools from the sulphurous spring
in a bubble of freedom, my fifty-fourth birthday,
in rooftop baths, by the gulls' wavering.

How hard she works, my dark Grecian daughter,
hands clenched on the wheel, quick glint of her rings,
marriage, new job. How heavily water,
oiled by the sulphur, smoothes each winter limb.
Roman pipes pump to a Celtic languor.
By rose-red chimneys, I rise and swim.

Sulis Minerva, they took both your names
into the dark which I fear will come back.
When you rose into daylight, girls' eyes shone the same
with shivering shoulders which longed for the south.
With rough hair of weed, eyes sunken and black,
water, not word, wash us warm through your mouth.

Diary of a stretcher bearer

Harry Scott was not a child, though he neatly wrote of tea.
In a 'palace' of a liner he steamed to Gallipoli,
he glimpsed the veiled women, then the deep dark blue of sea.

Harry Scott heard live men screaming, saw their beds torn by a shell,
through fever, steak and onion, he moved to a different hell,
tin hats leaned, staked in French mud, 'with a small poor cross as well'.

Gassed, Harry left his diary, blinded temporarily,
married his nurse to watch her, over thirty years, pour tea.
Did each dream stir dead men, calling? Did he taste the dark blue sea?

Stubbs and the horse

Stubbs' paintings hang still in the cool gallery
(three bombs shut the Tate). As I led my pony
I twisted my foot; swelling hid the fanned bone.
Unsound, I skim catalogues, coolly, at home.
For eighteen months Stubbs camped in a farmhouse,
aided by Mary, aged fifteen, his 'niece'.

For his *Anatomy* (tendons, nerves, bones),
he slaughtered his horses, slit the hot vein.
After the gallons of blood had pumped through,
she hauled up each carcass. Stubbs carved, then drew.

But even half-skinned, each horse keeps its blaze,
trots on, brisk skeleton, apples for knees,
pelvis a cave, each bulged muscle a hill
glossed as black agate, stinking but still.
Here are the hunters, the racers the rich
poured cash through like water. These horses will live.

So Stubbs, with his wild strong Mary, survived
off the Marquess' stallion, mares with bright eyes,
improbable hills (lions were a mistake)
but nobody praised the enamels he baked,
their colours still pure. When the Prince broke his faith
Stubbs painted the huge bay, after its race.

The canvas is filled by its plunging dark back.
The horse had been whipped. The trainer was sacked.
The patron's power is the horse's alone.
The muscles are hills. There is pain in the bone.
The stableboy crouches. The owner refused
to pay Stubbs a pound. Stubbs successfully sued.

Poor, he retired, for years pondered bones,
died wrapped in his gown, in his silence, alone.
The mares glow like guineas. Their flanks hold the heat
of the hands curled on dusk in a Bloomsbury street.

John Wesley's horse

Riding from barn door to beach,
John Wesley practised what he preached.

Though horses were tight-reined in town
he let his own stretch its neck down,
to snatch, on clifftops, clover, thyme,
frail rose and tooth-brown dandelion.

John Wesley, I face deeper night.
I stare into the same blind light.
I wish you, in the empty hearse,
your horse's heaven. You could do worse.

Rosie

You block the slope, chestnut and truculent.
When you came, a gangling two-year-old,
you spotted me at once.
My muddy coat was rich with mints;
heart, with foolish love of horses.

My own horse hated you,
since you were turned out with the foal,
her foster-child. You were her distant cousin.
At twenty-two, she spotted her young rival,
without her fine socks; with a pale blonde mane
which, grazing, combed moon daisies. Effortless.

How the old hate the young. How the young pine.
Once you pawed the wire fence, hooked your front shoe,
yet hurtled over, unhurt, my true cob.
I should have bobbed through April's woods on you,
have bolted in the blurring stubble field,
sweated, cursed, forgot. Horses are love

but love is for the young and I am old,
my right hip's stabbing held at bay by pills.
My old mare, curled beside the water trough,
sleeps like a warm dog. How did you make
scuffs on your polished forehead? Still half-broken,
you have been advertised. You are for sale.
This is your chance.

We smell the mints' perfume
blow from my pocket. The tiny crescent moon
rides on your shoulder. The deer stir in the woods,
the swifts surge higher. But I take my course
down the rough grasses, in the heat's last haze.
You are not my horse.

Take off

Rough stubble glows, burnt apricot.
A buzzard soars. Light clings.
His breast a travelling sunset,
he warms the world with wings.

Harvest

It was the year of flood and stinking mud.
But plums hung huge, as warm as blood,

so full of rain they fell into the mouth
then drank all thirst through hours of drought.

Pumps hummed. Wasps let the darkening purple stay,
bloom to the sun's mist at the end of day.

Though roses snag your wrist, your tender lobe,
stretch to a plum. Reach down the ruined globe.

In an August garden

Where, I asked, did the spiders come
suspended huge and still,
as skies cooled and the dews grew long,
backs printed with a skull?
Where were they when sun burned my crown,
I slashed the browning roses down?
I dare not lean through borders lest
I spin them out through homeless air,
unlink their glistening nets.

This year, I saw. Crumpled and gold
crammed in a fold of leaf
small spiders swarmed across my hands,
spilled to the ground beneath.
Then came the first web, braving rain,
the centred spider, one brown grain.
So spiders do not come. They grow.
Wind shivers worn skin. Now I know,
I must ask where the spiders go.

At Needlehole

How lovely the land lies in October,
still as the moon.
The new wheat is planted.
The drivers are gone
to pile up their wood
or be soothed by a screen.

The felled tree is sawn,
the robin's cross cry
now liquid and long,
uncannily high.
The cold finds my fingers.
The moon finds the sky.

The nymph considers the garden

If you pull all groundsel out of your beds,
hide the towers of plant pots under the shed,
throw out six cracked buckets, the babies' bath,
tie back the tall phlox, whose petals flood paths,
prune purple sage, which invades every lawn,
clear stumps, where the woodpecker cackles at dawn,
you will have a fine plot, tidied and hacked.
Neighbours will love you. I will not come back.

The jobbing welder

He was the biker you employed,
ex-Navy, who stormed down the road
with chrome, blue steel, all uninsured,
when work came, always missing.

Each girlfriend ended with a crash.
Her flat, the compensation cash
lasted six months, but when at last
the child came, he went missing.

There was the quick black hole of drink,
new barmaids' faces, rings' changed glint.
I wear his boiler suits. I think
half of each zip was missing.

He left, in debt, botched racing cars,
bought a Ferrari. In whose bar
did someone brush him, with fierce eyes,
each shred of kindness missing?

He pawned his rings. The house was gone.
He flew to Venice, glimpsed his son.
Another boy hacked him from the beam
after he went missing.

His friends poured Stella on his grave.
From the workbench, as though he lived,
tools disappear. All that you need,
all that you love, goes missing.

The button factory in Bologna

I throw the final buttons in the tray.
They rattle, bone on bone, the hollow day,
the dusk I drink in. No one knows me here.
I knot my rosy shawl. Strip twenty years:
'I won't sing that! It is too plain.' Then Handel
flung up the sash, grabbed my waist, let me dangle
above the rushing street. 'I am Beelzebub,
you devil!' Onioned breath. How close to love
hate runs. How close my singing came to war.
I scratched my rival, drank my crowd's applause.

Yes, I did think the men would never leave.
But I was choosy with the flowers they gave.
I threw the lilies at them. 'This room stinks.'
I took no cottage trash, Sweet Williams, pinks.
I wanted roses, with their greedy crowns'
rich pollen, sharp leaves, petals tumbling down.
I wanted armfuls, scattered on each bed.
But breasts are fat, voice, muscle. Now, instead
of lovers, I drain drinks. I gave up all
wine for a week, for my rose-printed shawl.

Did thick books tell you, I threw all away?
I laugh like gulls. This town tonight hangs grey
as your dull ports. Listen. I hear the ice
crack like my boots. Your tastes will not stay nice
when coasts flood, wires go down. I drank the worth
of one small voice. You threw away the earth.

That is your business. I will carry on,
hungover, silent in the women's song.
The shawl waits on its hook. And I would say
mine are the finest buttons in the tray.

Loosely based on the life of Francesca Cuzzoni, one of Handel's most
difficult divas, who became a factory worker.

The Beatles in Hamburg

I was a child, they were grown;
now I am grown, and three were dead.
The German girl who watched them said
'Boys in leather! Beautiful boys!'

She loved the one who turned his back
upon the crowd, painted all night,
murmured 'So sorry' – then collapsed.
The flier pays the fare for flight.

I love the ones they never were.
There was a man in Liverpool
who told them, like rough boys at school,
to wear French suits and trim their hair.

They could not stay in those wet streets
where prostitutes would lean and yawn,
the filthy room with flags for quilts,
the raucous laugh, the German dawn.

I cannot stay too late. One song
ripped and roared into their ears,
caught – Lennon mourned – the Hamburg years
when war seemed over, night stretched long,
but peace lay short-lived. Play that song.

The group then included Stuart Sutcliffe, who died in Germany. The track
singled out by John Lennon was 'I Saw Her Standing There'.

Mentioned in Minnesota

And funnel cake. 'Now what is that?'
'You pour the batter into fat
down a long funnel. It is Dutch;
fry, roll in sugar, eat it hot.
It is fair food.' In noise and frost,
crusts' sugar thick enough to choke,
doughnuts, that spun like Saturn's rings,
have floated me through bonfire smoke.

Some cakes are lost. Glossed black with seed,
the one grandfather's mother made
plump, widow-sharp with caraway,
though re-created, shrank and greyed.
Some cakes are found. I tasted one
from a married woman's hand,
gift to my husband, honey rich.
I stole the recipe and planned.

I could not taste my mother's sponge
without feeling the Fifties plunge
prim as white sugar. Passion cake
brings coffee-shops, the lover's lunge.
The Celts knew cakes: the long flapjacks,
treacle, like winter sun, oozed through.
A landlady brought frail drop scones
in Scotland's west, where fuchsias blew.

Which is the one I choose to make?
On Christmas Eve, a chocolate cake,
four eggs, heaped cocoa, beaten hard –
one hour until the domed crust breaks.
Milk buttons, walnuts, make its crown,
black cherries ooze. I taste feast's day,
a single slice, wrap dark fruit in
the bag my daughter bears away.

Getting up

At the entrance to my dream I met the author.
I had no time to tell
if he was pleased with his creation.
He ran from it like hell
with his old coat, his battered Leica.
I think he wished me well.

Wilfred Owen at the Advanced Horse Transport Depot, 1917

based on his letters

These are the best days I have ever had
since I enlisted, with the frostbite gone
melted with nights I thought I would go mad

into the horses, solid as their muck.
One leapt as I got on. Somehow I sat
each stiff-legged buck.

Then we bowled four horse wagons through the frost.
We passed the fields of Crécy, blind with light.
Nothing is lost.

A boy, I galloped Scarborough's sand. The dance
of hooves beat in my head. My long back sore,
I pound white roads of France.

How horses jar us, scar us, yet our rest
falls sweet as their oats' hiss.
Let my days pour.
These are the best.

5 a.m.

It tapped against my window. I am wind.
I swept the frosted paper from your tap.
I blew the birds, for berries, from the steppe.

I sent the deer running in vast herds.
I rounded up the stars. Now I have hurled
snow in the gutters, train doors, motorways,
the vast dome of a dustbin lid. Your tracks
run small as mice across your altered world.

First

First snow flies at me like a flower.
Have I risked snow on a bike before?
First snow flies at me like a flower.

Fine ice grains grate into my eyes.
I wonder how the horses are.
Fine ice grains grate into my eyes.

They spend two hours upon the hill,
trudge ice, as horses rush away,
they spend two hours upon the hill

as whitened heels drum into dark,
as horses glimpse wolves, drifts, the end,
as whitened heels drum into dark.

How old these horses are. High gods,
their massive necks sweep back-lit doors,
how old these horses are. High gods

the perfect crystals gleam, and blow,
the red lights fade. The drowned stars go.
The perfect crystals bloom and blow.

The twenty-ninth of December

There is no blossom on the plum.
There is no fruit left, red or black.
But glowing like a rosy torch
although it stole both fruit and flower
the bullfinch, lured by seed, bobs back.

Looking for the cat

It is the time of night when the blood slows
the time of cold when steel grinds in the locks
the time of moon which wakes, on street's dark side,
the distant icy barking of the fox.

In store

Twelve days of frost, and the heart slows.
The fingers stretch to smallest things,
find one warm towel, the last red hip
left startled on the straggling rose.

With skin grown black as leathers, spice,
left in the shed, bananas freeze.
Their tips, where flower flared, glimmer ice.
Flesh melts to honey, paradise.

FLOOD

1
Flood

We are made of water. But we forgot.
For twelve long hours the sky sank down like lead
without a breath of wind. Rain's rush swept slates.
Offices dripped; you broke for home, instead
of cycling, seemed to swim. Drains gaped like graves,
iron lids askew. Cars breasted tidal waves,

one road, brown flood, one, water spouts. Yet this
was the storm's lull. Huddled in café's steam
'I've never seen such floods in thirty years'
travellers gulped down all hopes of reaching home.
As the winds rose, to dry phones' sweet sea bells
they left for schoolfriends, cousins, hot hotels.

Then came the panic. For the pumps were drowned.
In wastes of water, taps would soon run dry.
Then people fought in queues across the town
as bottled water, glittering, swept by
on rain-soaked pallets, for the rain was sharp
as ice. Cars loaded. Then the shops fell dark.

Your gleaming tap coughed empty to the sink.
Surge reached the Abbey, kissed the dead in graves.
You sat by a few pints you dared not drink.
You wished, like your deep fathers, you had saved.
Yet the Ark held. Washed empty by your day
you let the dark's flood carry you away.

2
Mitchell

Yes, I can see him. He is just nineteen,
as we were nineteen. Ducking out the bar,

bravo, he lights a cigarette. The gleam
warms his untouched cheeks, as to a mother,

the tender hollows of his collarbone.
Floods murmur everywhere. He tells the others

he knows the field paths, he is walking home.
What do they hear in dark? A branch's crack,

a child's cry. 'I don't know how to swim.'
They have no lights, no rope to haul on slack,

the hidden stream pulls stronger than a horse.
Dark sweeps him on. Day cannot bring him back.

Ten miles downstream, I hack at storm's stunned flowers,
brush down one whole but thin-stemmed rose, toss it

into a pail, so I may lose no hours
of its small breaths, honey and apricot.

Buoyed on the loose soft rainwater, it swirls.
Radio's tides wash over my calm bucket.

'A body found in Tewkesbury in fields
has not yet been identified.' But far

in Stroud, in Slad, in Gloucester's cloud, young girls,
the old men name you, see you as you are

never again. Rose ash falls from your fingers,
the wet door clicks. You walk into the bar.

3

Bowsers

'Boozer' writes Confused of Gloucester.
Dazed by screens, I mutter 'Browser' –
No. They are bowsers. When I first
glimpsed one squat blue tank, I reversed,
leaned over it, not to ease thirst,
but to admire its taps' brass shimmer,
hissed and spun, its water's glitter.

For two days it stood mainly dry.
On most trips, rattling bottles by
to shops, hill springs, I leant in vain.
Young women walked as to a shrine,
swung buckets slowly, stood in line.
Grandmother's grandfather, I know,
could poise two buckets on his yoke.
Not spill one drop – and light his pipe.

Three ageless women camped on chairs,
guarded their tank. 'You're not from here,
you can't have this.' Then water flowed,
the north-west's tankers blocked our road,
throbbed bedroom panes the yellow moon rode.
We touched the taps. Cool gushed beneath
quick as love's spasms, dear as breath.

I spot them now with gaiety.
'A white one, look, from Scotland! "Dee"' –
Soldiers hand bottles to hug home.
We need not run when tankers come.
Yet I fear, as the waters hiss,
I need not tell grandchildren this.
They will know what a bowser is.

4
Litres

You can brush your teeth in one gulp of water
from a clean bottle. You can wash your hair

in one rich litre, catch it in a bowl;
rinse out two blouses, let the good suds flow

into the hungry cistern. Haul the tank
out of the workshop, rig a water bank

where rain sweeps the shed roof, though you must go
two hours in storms, to bale the overflow.

You can drive to the farm, where limestone's cool
pumps private pipelines. With your bottles full

they laugh to see you scramble through the moss
to wrench the tap, so not one drop is lost.

You see Range Rovers where the camp-gear gleams,
then council tenants, scrambling to their streams.

Your kitchen creeps to boil, you cannot think,
back aches, clouds sink to heaven. You can drink.

5
Switched on

After eight days, the taps gush out.
Unwashed, I find the small shops packed,
children with sweets and squeals.
Each head is soaked, sleeked black.
I bob amongst a colony of seals.

6
Review

We were not flooded. On our routes
land stinks of carpet, rotten fruit,
Ashchurch, Tewkesbury.

Tide stopped two inches from our power,
the petrol pumps, the shops' rich bower,
Painswick, Coberley.

Cholera swam in that brown tide.
Yet people lived, unharmed, beside,
Twyning, Ledbury.

We were an island, heard elsewhere
farm water pump, full washers purr,
Newent, St Briavel.

Now, though the water fades by night,
though cracked mains spill, it will come right
in Gloucester, Quedgeley, Tuffley.

I cry like water. Do not hope.
Switch off, then walk. Refuse to cope
in Hatherley, Hawling, Whaddon.

The rivers rise, the doomed pumps hum,
the walls are down, the waters come
to Munich, Paris, London.

No

No one is ever good enough,
or kind enough.
No one stays awake
through the lovely rush of rain which fills our dark.
No one can hold the music.
They are counting coins or frowning,
they are toppling, they are drowning.
No one is good.

But nothing is as quick as us,
no screen can match us,
tape's whirr catch us,
nothing tilts like sun
to light from sad.
Nothing in all history
can reach to take your hand from me,
the dark, the rain's gift, O
we should be glad.

Acknowledgements

Grateful thanks to the editors of the following publications, in which some of these poems first appeared: *Agenda, Artemis, The Bow-Wow Shop, The Chimaera, The Flea, Handel News, Hearing Voices, Horizon, The John Clare Society Journal, The London Magazine, Magma, Mimesis, Modern Poetry in Translation, The North, nthWORD, Other Poetry, PN Review, Poetry London, Poetry Review, Poetry Wales, The Reader, The Rialto, Scintilla, Shadow, Snakeskin, Stand, Staple, The Times Literary Supplement, The Warwick Review, The Yellow Nib; The Forward Book of Poetry 2011* (Faber, 2010), *Night Shift* (Five Leaves, 2010), *No Space But Their Own* (ed. Joy Howard, Grey Hen Press, 2010), *Of Love and Hope* (ed. Deborah Gaye, Avalanche, 2010), *Poems in the Waiting Room* (2009), *The RSPB Anthology of Wildlife Poems* (ed. Celia Warren, A. & C. Black, 2011), *Seductive Harmonies* (ed. Deborah Gaye, Avalanche, 2012), *Seeking Refuge* (ed. Jan Fortune-Wood, Cinnamon, 2010), *Shadow* (HappenStance, 2009), *Pendulum* (ed. Deborah Gaye, Avalanche, 2007); and thanks to BBC Radio 3.